ADVANTAGE Test Prep 1

MW00806055

Table of Contents

Introduction 3

Reading

Introduction to Reading 6
Nonfiction Reading Selection: *All About Weather* 7
Vocabulary
High-Frequency Words 8
Phonograms 9
Comprehension
Main Idea 10
Fantasy and Realism 11
Compare and Contrast 12
Fiction Reading Selection: *Do We Have To?* 13
Reading for Details 14
Drawing Conclusions 15
Categorizing and Classifying 16
Retelling in Order 17
Poetry Reading Selection: "Weather" 18
Making Predictions 19
Making Inferences 20
Responding to Reading 21
Graphic Information
Map Reading 22
Charts and Graphs 23
Calendars 24
Forms 25
Reference Sources
Alphabet Skills 26
Using a Dictionary 27
Environmental Print 28
Using a Library 29

Writing

Introduction to Writing: Understanding Writing Prompts . . 30
Understanding Scoring Rubrics 31
Prewriting 32
Writing Prompt and Checklist 33
Plan Your Writing 34
Write Your First Draft 35
Revise Your Writing 37

Language

Introduction to Language 39
Mechanics
Sentences 40
Periods 41
Question Marks 42
Exclamation Points 43
Capitalizing Names 44
Grammar and Usage
Nouns 45
Describing Words 46
Verbs 47
Present Tense 48
Past Tense 49
Complete and Incomplete Sentences 50
Singular and Plural Nouns 51
Possessives 52
Spelling
Spelling the /k/ Sound 53
Spelling Common Words 54

Table of Contents

Introduction to Mathematics 55

Number Sense and Numeration

Counting 56

Which Is More?. 57

Number Order. 58

Computation, Operations, Estimation

Counting On to Add. 59

Counting Back to Subtract 60

Fact Families 61

Ordinal Numbers 62

Odd and Even Numbers. 63

Number Sentences 64

Which Sign? 65

Place Value 66

Counting Dimes, Nickels,
    and Pennies 67

Estimating 68

Geometry

Comparing Shapes 69

Counting Sides 70

Symmetry. 71

Measurement

Measuring Length 72

Measuring Weight 73

Telling Time 74

Patterns and Relationships

Number Patterns 75

Graphing

Reading a Graph 76

Problem Solving

Making a Plan. 77

Showing Your Work 78

Practice Test Introduction 79

Practice Test: Reading. 80

Practice Test: Writing 88

Practice Test: Language. 94

Practice Test: Math 99

Answer Key 108

CREDITS

Concept Development: Kent Publishing Services, Inc.

Written by: Linda Barr and Michael Silverstone

Editor: Carla Hamaguchi

Designer: Moonhee Pak

Illustrator: Jenny Campbell

Art Director: Tom Cochrane

Project Director: Carolea Williams

© 2004 Creative Teaching Press, Inc., Huntington Beach, CA 92649

Reproduction of activities in any manner for use in the classroom and not for commercial sale is permissible.
Reproduction of these materials for an entire school or for a school system is strictly prohibited.

Introduction

Testing is a big part of education today, and this workbook is designed to help students become better prepared to succeed at taking standardized and proficiency tests. This workbook contains skills and strategies that can be used in any kind of testing situation. Even if students don't have to take standardized tests, they will still benefit from studying the skills and strategies in this workbook.

Standardized Tests

Standardized tests get their name because they are administered in the exact same way to hundreds of thousands of students across the country. They are also referred to as *norm-referenced tests*. Norms give educators a common standard of measurement of students' skills and abilities across the country. Students are ranked according to their test scores and then assigned a percentile ranking. This ranking tells what percent of all students scored better or worse than the norm.

Proficiency Tests

Many states develop their own statewide proficiency tests. Proficiency tests are also known as *criterion-referenced tests*. This means that the test is based on a list of standards and skills (criteria). States develop standards for what students should know at each grade level. The proficiency test evaluates how well students have mastered these standards.

Although both tests may look similar, they measure different things. A proficiency test measures a student's mastery of set standards. A standardized test compares a student's achievement to others who took the same test across the country.

Many tests were reviewed in developing the material for this workbook. They include the following:
- **California Achievement Tests (CAT)**
- **Comprehensive Tests of Basic Skills (CTBS)**
- **TerraNova**
- **Iowa Tests of Basic Skills (ITBS)**
- **Metropolitan Achievement Tests (MAT)**
- **Stanford Achievement Tests (SAT)**
- **Texas Assessment of Knowledge and Skills (TAKS)**

It is important to recognize that all national standardized achievement tests work essentially the same way. They ask multiple-choice questions, have specific time limits, and compare your child's results to national averages. The goal of this test-prep series is to teach **test-taking strategies** so that no matter which test your child is required to take, he or she will be successful.

Introduction

Preparing for Tests

The more students are prepared for taking standardized and proficiency tests, the better they will do on those tests. A student who understands the skills commonly measured and who practices test-taking strategies will be more likely to be a successful test-taker. The more the student knows and knows what to expect, the more comfortable he or she will be in actual test-taking situations.

Standardized and proficiency testing is used to:

- evaluate students' progress, strengths, and weaknesses.
- show how each student's school achievement compares with other students on a local and nationwide level (standardized).
- show an individual student's achievement of set standards (proficiency).
- select students for remedial or achievement programs.
- tell educators whether school systems are succeeding.
- evaluate the success of school programs.
- help educators develop programs to suit their students' specific needs.

Standardized tests are only one measure of student achievement, however. Teachers use many other methods to gain insights into each student's skills, abilities, and knowledge. They evaluate students through day-to-day observation, evaluation, and assessment.

Introduction

How Can Parents Help Children Suceed at Standardized Testing?

The following list includes suggestions on how to prepare your child for testing.

Tips for Parents

- Monitor your child's progress.
- Get to know your child's teacher, and find out what he or she thinks you can do to help your child at home.
- Be informed about your state's testing requirements.
- Motivate your child to prepare.
- Make homework part of your child's daily routine.
- Set aside a period of time each day to study with your child.
- Read aloud to your child.
- Share learning experiences with your child.
- Make sure your child is getting the sleep and nutrition he or she needs to succeed.
- Always nurture your child's curiosity and desire to learn.
- Encourage your child to learn about computers and technology.
- Encourage your child to take tests very seriously but to have healthy expectations and keep testing in perspective.
- Offer encouragement and support so that your child wants to make a good effort.

Where Can I Learn More About Testing?

ERIC Clearinghouse on Assessment and Evaluation
209 O'Boyle Hall
The Catholic University of America
Washington, DC 20064
(202) 319-5120
http://ericae.net/

National Center for Fair and Open Testing, Inc. (FairTest)
342 Broadway
Cambridge, MA 02139
http://www.fairtest.org/

Introduction to Reading

Reading is an important part of life and one of the most vital skills required for success on standardized and proficiency tests as well as in many careers. The best way for children to improve reading skills is to become avid readers. The most successful readers read for pleasure. They tend to read often, with others and alone. They read many different types of materials as a natural habit. The more children read, the more fluent they become. This tends to make reading more rewarding. Research has found a direct connection between the amount of time a child reads and high academic performance as measured on tests.

Nearly every standardized or proficiency test includes a section on reading. The reading passages may be fiction, nonfiction, or poetry. They may also be graphic information like maps or reference information like library catalog cards and dictionaries. Students are asked to recall, interpret, and reflect on what they read.

The following pages give a review of reading skills. They allow students to practice the skills with questions just like the ones they will be expected to answer on tests. In this workbook section, students will prepare for questions that ask them to:

- explain the meanings of **common (high-frequency) words.**

- distinguish among **rhyming words (phonograms).**

- identify the **main idea.**

- tell the difference between **fantasy and realism.**

- **compare and contrast** two things.

- identify **details** in a reading selection.

- **draw conclusions** from what an author has written.

- **classify or categorize** items into groups.

- **retell** the events in a selection in chronological order.

- **make predictions** about what will happen next.

- **make inferences** by applying ideas to life in general.

- **respond to a reading** with personal opinions.

- understand **graphic information** such as maps, graphs, calendars, and forms.

- use **reference skills** such as knowing how to use libraries and dictionaries.

Advantage Test Prep Grade 1 © 2004 Creative Teaching Press

All About Weather

What makes the wind blow? It's the sun! The sun warms the land and the water. Then heat from the land and water warms the air. Some places get warmer than others.

As air warms, it moves up. Then cold air comes to take its place. When the cold air comes, we feel wind.

What makes rain and snow fall? It's the sun again! Some air carries tiny bits of water. The sun warms this air. It rises into the sky and cools off.

The tiny bits of water cool off, too. They group together. They become larger drops of water. These water drops form clouds.

The drops keep getting larger and heavier. Then they are too heavy to stay in the sky. They fall as rain.

In winter, the air in the clouds is very cold. The drops of water turn into drops of ice. When the drops of ice get too heavy, they fall. This time, they are snow.

Without the sun, we would not have weather!

Reading

KNOW THE SKILL: **High-Frequency Words**

You will read some words over and over. When you don't know a word, read the other words around it. Look at the pictures. Then you might know what it is.

Test Example

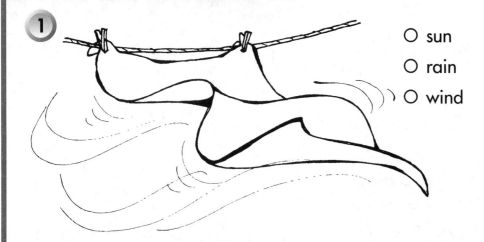

1

- ○ sun
- ○ rain
- ○ wind

Think About the Answer

The answer is *wind.* Wind is blowing the sheet. The picture does not show the sun or rain. It does show a sheet, but *sheet* is not one of the choices.

Now You Try It

2

- ○ warm
- ○ cold
- ○ drop

Check your answer on page 108.

Advantage Test Prep Grade 1 © 2004 Creative Teaching Press

Vocabulary

KNOW THE SKILL: **Phonograms**

If one word looks like another word, say it aloud. Look at the first letter. Check the last letter. Look at the picture and choose the correct word.

Test Example

 1

- ○ rain
- ○ pain
- ○ train

Think About the Answer

The answer is *rain.* All three words rhyme, but the picture shows rain. *Pain* means that something hurts. A *train* is a vehicle that runs on a track.

Now You Try It

 2

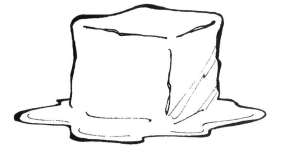

- ○ school
- ○ cool
- ○ tool

Check your answer on page 108.

KNOW THE SKILL: **Main Idea**

The most important idea is the main idea. It is what the writer wants you to remember. The main idea is often in the first sentence.

Test Example

1 What was *All About Weather* about?

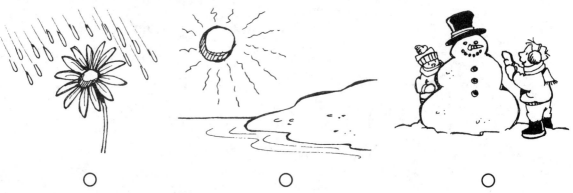

○   ○   ○

Think About the Answer

The second picture shows a main idea from the passage. The sun warms the water and land, causing wind. The passage did not talk about rain making flowers grow. It also did not tell about building a snowman.

Now You Try It

2 Which picture shows another main idea from *All About Weather*?

○   ○   ○

Check your answer on page 108.

Comprehension

Reading

KNOW THE SKILL: **Fantasy and Realism**

Some stories are about real things. Others are make-believe. As you read, ask yourself if the things in the story could have really happened. Or did someone make them up?

Test Example

 1   Which can really happen?

○   ○   ○

Think About the Answer

The last picture shows something that can really happen. Real clouds do not have faces, so the first and second pictures are make-believe, not real.

Now You Try It

 2   Which is make-believe?

○   ○   ○

Check your answer on page 108.

KNOW THE SKILL: **Compare and Contrast**

A question might ask how two things are the same or how they are different. Here's an example: A cat and a dog are both animals with fur, four feet, and a tail. They are different, though; dogs bark, while cats meow.

Test Example

1 Which shows that rain and snow are alike?

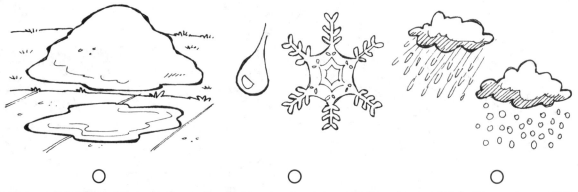

○　　　　　　　　　　○　　　　　　　　　　○

Think About the Answer

The third picture is correct. It shows that rain and snow both come from clouds. The first and second pictures show how rain and snow are different. The first picture shows that rain forms a puddle, while snow forms a pile. The second picture shows that rain is liquid drops of water, while snow is frozen crystals of water.

Now You Try It

2 Is this a similarity or a difference? The sun is round and so is the moon.

_____

Check your answer on page 108.

Do We Have To?

Grandfather came to live with Luis and his mother. They live in Iowa. He used to live in Mexico. At first, Grandfather spoke only Spanish. Now Luis is teaching him English. It is fun!

The only problem is dinnertime. Every night, Mama serves rice and beans with dinner! Luis is getting tired of them.

After dinner, Luis always helps clean up. "Mama, do we have to eat rice and beans every night?" he asks. "Doesn't Grandfather like anything else?"

"Luis, do you remember that I used to live in Mexico with Grandfather?" Mama asks. Luis nods. That was long ago.

"We had very little money then. We could not buy meat. Still, we never went to bed hungry. We ate rice and beans every night. They helped us grow. They kept us strong. Without rice and beans, I might not be here."

Luis gives Mama a big hug. "Let's have rice and beans again tomorrow, okay?"

KNOW THE SKILL: **Reading for Details**

You may be asked to choose the detail that answers a question. Details tell more about the main idea.

Test Example

 1 Who just moved from Mexico?

O Luis

O his mother

O Grandfather

Think About the Answer

Grandfather moved from Mexico. We do not know if Luis ever lived in Mexico. Mama lived in Mexico long ago.

Now You Try It

 2 What is Luis teaching his grandfather?

_____

_____

Check your answer on page 108.

Advantage Test Prep Grade 1 © 2004 Creative Teaching Press

Comprehension

Reading

KNOW THE SKILL: **Drawing Conclusions**

Writers tell you some things in a story. You can make decisions about other things by yourself. After you read a story, think about what you read and what you know.

Test Example

1. Why does Mama make rice and beans every night?

- ○ She has no money.
- ○ She is just learning how to cook.
- ○ Grandfather likes rice and beans.

Think About the Answer

The third choice is correct. Mama wants Grandfather to be happy, so she cooks what he likes. Mama talks about not having money in Mexico, but that was long ago. The story does not say that Mama is just learning how to cook.

Now You Try It

2. Why does Luis ask Mama to make rice and beans?

_____

_____

_____

Check your answer on page 108.

Comprehension

KNOW THE SKILL: **Categorizing and Classifying**

When you categorize and classify, you put things in groups. You might group things by color, shape, size, or something else.

Test Example

1 In which group would you put rice and beans?

○   ○   ○

Think About the Answer

Rice and beans is a kind of food, so it belongs in the second group, with other kinds of food. The first group is clothing. Rice and beans is not a kind of clothing. The third group is animals. Rice and beans is not a kind of animal.

Now You Try It

2 What is the best name for this group of people?

○ family
○ helpers
○ neighbors

Check your answer on page 108.

Advantage Test Prep Grade 1 © 2004 Creative Teaching Press

KNOW THE SKILL: **Retelling in Order**

When you retell a story, you tell things in the same order that the story did. As you read, remember the order.

Test Example

 Which happened FIRST?

○   ○   ○

Think About the Answer

The story started with Luis teaching Grandfather to say some words in English. That means the third picture came first. It is the correct answer. Luis ate rice and beans later. Even later, Luis helped clean up.

Now You Try It

2 Which happened LAST?

○   ○   ○

Check your answer on page 108.

Weather

by Anonymous

Whether the weather be fine,
Or whether the weather be not,
Whether the weather be cold,
Or whether the weather be hot,
We'll weather the weather
Whatever the weather,
whether we like it or not!

Advantage Test Prep Grade 1 © 2004 Creative Teaching Press

Reading

KNOW THE SKILL: **Making Predictions**

After you read a story or poem, think about what happened. Then you can guess what might happen next.

Test Example

1 What would the poet do during a rain storm?

 ○    ○    ○

Think About the Answer

A storm would not stop her from taking her trip. The answer is the second picture. It shows her getting on a bus. The first and third pictures show her staying home. She would probably not do that.

Now You Try It

2 What would the poet do if she had to write a letter?

 ○    ○    ○

Check your answer on page 108.

KNOW THE SKILL: Making Inferences

Writers do not tell you everything. Look for clues that help you figure out for yourself what happened.

Test Example

1 Where does the poet live?

◯   ◯   ◯

Think About the Answer

The poem says that weather can be cold or hot. That clue means that the third picture shows where she lives. In the first picture, the weather is always hot. In the second picture, the weather is always cold.

Now You Try It

2 What kind of person is the poet?

◯   ◯   ◯

Check your answer on page 108.

KNOW THE SKILL: **Responding to Reading**

When you read a poem or story, think about how it makes you feel. Let it make pictures in your mind. Think of specific reasons for your feelings.

Test Example

1 How do you feel about weather? Do you feel the same way about weather as this poet? Explain your answer.

_____

_____

_____

Think About the Answer

You might have said that you are not bothered by the weather either. Or you might have said that you are happy if it's sunny and you are sad if it's rainy. However you answered, you should have explained your reasons.

Now You Try It

2 What did you like about the poem?

_____

_____

_____

Check your answer on page 108.

Reading

KNOW THE SKILL: **Map Reading**

Some tests will ask you questions about a map. Read the words on the map. Look for arrows that show the directions. *N* stands for *north*. *S* stands for *south*, *W* stands for *west*, and *E* stands for *east*.

Test Example

1. From the United States, which direction is Mexico?

   ○ north
   ○ south
   ○ west

Canada

United States

Pacific Ocean

Atlantic Ocean

Mexico

Gulf of Mexico

N
W ◉ E
S

Think About the Answer

Mexico is below the United States on the map. The arrow that points down is labeled *S*, for *south*. The correct answer is *south*. Canada is north. The Pacific Ocean is west.

Now You Try It

2. Which answer correctly completes the sentence?

   _____ is west of Mexico.

   ○ The United States
   ○ The Pacific Ocean
   ○ The Gulf of Mexico

Check your answer on page 108.

Graphic Information

Reading

KNOW THE SKILL: **Charts and Graphs**

Charts and graphs are ways to share information. On this graph, the days of the week run across the bottom. The temperature is on the left side. The line across the chart shows the temperature for each day of the week.

Test Example

1. What was the temperature on Tuesday?

   ○ 58

   ○ 62

   ○ 68

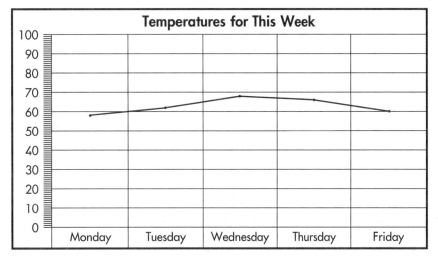

Think About the Answer

It was 62 on Tuesday. To find the temperature for Tuesday, put your finger on the name of the day. Then move your finger to the top of the line. Look to the left side of the graph to read the 62.

Now You Try It

2. What was the hottest day this week?

   ○ Monday

   ○ Tuesday

   ○ Wednesday

Check your answer on page 108.

Graphic Information

Reading

KNOW THE SKILL: Calendars

Calendars show the days of the week. Each row across a calendar is seven days. The calendar below shows two weeks of a month. The names of the days are at the top. Each day has a number for the date. People write notes on calendars to remember important events.

Test Example

1 What day of the week is May 11?

○ Monday   ○ Wednesday   ○ Friday

May

Sunday	Monday	Tuesday	Wednesday	Thursday	Friday	Saturday
1	2	3	4	5 Kaylee's birthday	6	7
8	9	10 Dr. Brown 4:15	11	12	13 Field Trip at school	14

Think About the Answer

Find the box with 11 in it. Then look at the top of the row and see which day it is. *Wednesday* is the correct answer.

Now You Try It

2 When is Kaylee's birthday?

○ Tuesday, May 5

○ Tuesday, May 10

○ Thursday, May 5

Check your answer on page 108.

Advantage Test Prep Grade 1 © 2004 Creative Teaching Press

Reading

KNOW THE SKILL: **Forms**

Forms ask for information. You will fill out many forms in your life. Read forms carefully.

Test Example

Kim Sampson is 6. She lives with her mother, Jennifer. Their phone number is 555-9819.

(1) What should Kim write on Line 4?

_____

Highlands Pool
Swim Lessons—Minnows

July 11–15, 10:00–10:40 a.m.

1) Name_____

2) Age _____

3) Address _____

4) Phone number_____

5) Name of parent or guardian _____

Think About the Answer

Line 4 asks for Kim's phone number. It is 555-9819.

Now You Try It

(2) What should Kim write on Line 5?

_____

Check your answer on page 109.

Reference Sources

KNOW THE SKILL: **Alphabet Skills**

Lists of words are often in ABC order. To put words in ABC order, look at the first letter of each word. The word that starts with the letter that comes first in the alphabet is first in ABC order. If two words start with the same letter, look at the second letter to know which comes first in ABC order.

Test Example

 1 Write these words in ABC order:

| book | tree | shirt | monkey |

Think About the Answer

The correct order is *book, monkey, shirt, tree* (b, m, s, t).

Now You Try It

 2 Write these words in ABC order:

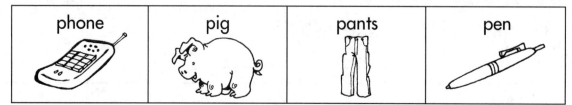

| phone | pig | pants | pen |

Check your answer on page 109.

Advantage Test Prep Grade 1 © 2004 Creative Teaching Press

Reference Sources

KNOW THE SKILL: **Using a Dictionary**

A dictionary is a book of words in ABC order. It tells what words mean and how to say them. The *guide words* printed at the top of the page are the first word and the last word on that page.

Test Example

1 Which guide words show that the word *neighbor* is on the page?

- ○ nap—noise
- ○ family—food
- ○ sister—squirrel

Think About the Answer

The first option is the correct answer. *Neighbor* starts with *n.* This pair of guide words starts with *n.* The second pair starts with *f.* The third pair starts with *s.*

Now You Try It

2 Which guide words show that the word *whistle* is on the page?

- ○ tool—tuna
- ○ warm—west
- ○ wheel—wise

Check your answer on page 109.

Reading

KNOW THE SKILL: **Environmental Print**

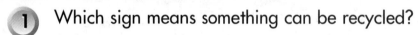

A test question might ask you to explain what a sign means. Think about where you have seen that sign.

Test Example

1. Which sign means something can be recycled?

○ ○ ○

Think About the Answer

When something is recycled, it's used again. The image of arrows making a circle means to use something again and again.

Now You Try It

2. Draw a sign that means stop.

Check your answer on page 109.

Advantage Test Prep Grade 1 © 2004 Creative Teaching Press

Reference Sources

Reading

KNOW THE SKILL: Using a Library

Most libraries list their books on computers. You might be looking for books on a certain subject. Then the computer may show a list of books from which you can choose.

Test Example

1. Which of these books might have a bear as the main character?

   _____

   _____

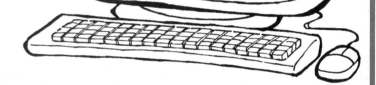

Bear's Weather by Harriet Ziefert
HarperCollins, 1993

Changing Climate by Sally Morgan
Franklin Watts, 1999

Weather Experiments with Everyday Materials by Muriel Mandell
Sterling Publishing, 1991

Think About the Answer

Bear's Weather sounds like a book about a bear.

Now You Try It

2. Which book would help you experiment with weather?

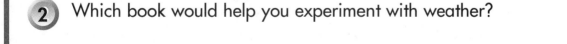

Check your answer on page 109.

Understanding Writing Prompts

On many tests, students will be asked to write about something. They will be given time to plan their writing, write, and revise their writing.

The writing section of a test has a special instruction called the **prompt.** It tells students what to write about. Here are some examples of the kinds of prompts that students might see on a writing test:

- Tell about a special day you had with a friend.

- Take a story you know. Write a new chapter for it.

- Pretend you are a character in a story you know. Write a letter to another character.

- Tell about a time you did something that made you feel proud.

- Describe someone you like or love.

- If you could be any animal, which one would you want to be? Give a few reasons why.

- Tell about a book you like. Say why you think it is a good book.

- Who do you look up to? Say why.

- Tell about something you value that doesn't cost money. Explain why it is valuable to you.

Students should read the writing prompt carefully and be sure to understand what it is asking. Here are some general tips for students to think about before they start to write:

- Try to see pictures in your mind and write what you see.

- If you are writing a story, introduce your characters by telling their names and saying what they are like at the beginning of your story.

- Give details that tell what things look like, sound like, smell like, and feel like.

- Think about books you like—it can be helpful to make your stories like the ones in those books.

- After you finish, read over what you wrote and see if you left out any words or ideas that you can add.

- When you think you are done, read over your writing again to check your spelling.

- Make sure sentences start with a capital letter and end with an end mark.

- In your final draft, make sure to form your letters neatly enough that someone else will have no trouble reading what you wrote.

The box below is called a **rubric.** Rubrics are used to score different parts of writing on a test. The numbers in this rubric have these meanings:

4	Excellent
3	Good
2	Just okay
1	Not good enough
0	Not really finished

Four areas in which your writing can be graded are explained below.

Part of Writing	Description	Score
Ideas	Do you have ideas to share with a reader?	
Organization	Does your writing move from part to part in a way a reader can understand?	
Sentence Structure	Are your sentences complete and easy to understand?	
Spelling, Punctuation, and Grammar	Can you spell first-grade spelling words correctly? Do your sentences start with a capital letter and end with a punctuation mark?	

Your writing will usually get a number grade (4, 3, 2, 1, or 0) in each of these areas. These numbers are added together to give a number score to your writing. When you evaluate your score by category, you will be able to see in which areas you need to improve.

Prewriting

On a test, a writing prompt will tell you your topic. You need to think of ideas about the topic. Here are two ways to get started:

Listing

Read the writing prompt below and write down all the words you can think of that relate to the topic. Later, you can choose the words or ideas you want to use. Here is one example:

Prompt: Tell about a time when you felt proud.

school play
a musical
my costume
learned my lines
Mom and Dad watched

Webbing

Make a "word web" of ideas. First, write the topic in the center circle. Then write ideas in the circles around the topic. You can add even smaller circles for details. The circles help you group ideas and details together.

Writing Prompt: Write about something you didn't think you could do—but you did.

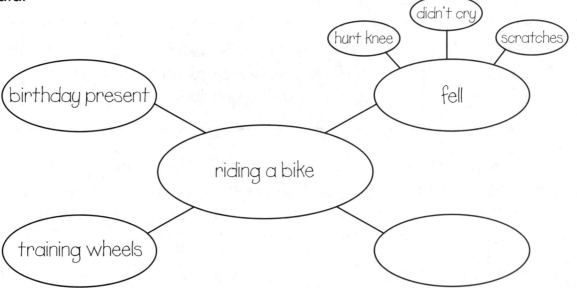

Advantage Test Prep Grade 1 © 2004 Creative Teaching Press

Writing Prompt and Checklist

Read the writing prompt below. Then read the checklist of tips that will help you do your best.

Writing Prompt

Tell about a skill you have, something you do well. Explain how you learned it. Tell why you are glad you can do this.

Writer's Checklist

Make sure you do all these things as you write:

- ☐ I named my skill.
- ☐ I told how I learned it. If someone helped me, I told who it was.
- ☐ I explained when and where I do this skill.
- ☐ I told why I am glad I have this skill.
- ☐ I used details to help explain my skill.
- ☐ My writing has a beginning, a middle, and an end.
- ☐ I have spelled first-grade spelling words right.
- ☐ I started names and the first word of each sentence with a capital letter.
- ☐ All of my sentences end with a period, a question mark, or an exclamation point.

Use this space to plan your writing. You can list your ideas or make a word web. You can also use another way to get started that works for you.

Advantage Test Prep Grade 1 © 2004 Creative Teaching Press

Write your first draft on the lines on pages 35 and 36.

_____

_____

_____

_____

_____

_____

_____

_____

_____

_____

_____

_____

_____

_____

_____

_____

Writing

_____

_____

_____

_____

_____

_____

_____

_____

_____

_____

_____

_____

_____

_____

_____

_____

_____

Use separate sheets of paper if you need more room.

Advantage Test Prep Grade 1 © 2004 Creative Teaching Press

Read what you wrote on pages 35 and 36. Now go back to the checklist on page 33. Did you do all the things on the list? Do you need to add ideas or details? Look for places to make your writing clearer. Check for spelling and other mistakes.

Then write your final draft below.

_____

_____

_____

_____

_____

_____

_____

_____

_____

_____

_____

_____

Writing

_____

_____

_____

_____

_____

_____

_____

Give Yourself a Score

Go back to the rubric on page 31. Give yourself a score from 4 to 0 for each category. Then ask someone else to score your writing. That way, you will have two scores.

How I Scored It

Ideas	Organization	Sentence Structure	Spelling, Punctuation, and Grammar
_____	_____	_____	_____

How Someone Else Scored It

Ideas	Organization	Sentence Structure	Spelling, Punctuation, and Grammar
_____	_____	_____	_____

 Advantage Test Prep Grade 1 © 2004 Creative Teaching Press

Many different language skills help us write and speak well. Some of the skills students can expect to see on a test are spelling, grammar, and punctuation.

One of the best ways to improve language skills is to read. Whenever we read, we learn how language is used. The more we read, the more it becomes part of us.

Here is a list of key skills students will learn and practice in this section:

- Sentences
- Periods
- Question Marks
- Exclamation Points
- Capitalizing Names
- Nouns
- Describing Words
- Verbs
- Present Tense
- Past Tense
- Complete and Incomplete Sentences
- Plurals
- Possessives
- Spelling

KNOW THE SKILL: **Sentences**

A sentence has a noun and a verb. The noun tells *who* and the verb tells *what*. A sentence begins with a capital letter. It ends with a period, a question mark, or an exclamation point.

Test Example

 1 Which is a sentence?

- ○ Stands tall.
- ○ Many red leaves.
- ○ The tree grew taller.

Think About the Answer

The third choice is a complete sentence. It names what the sentence is about: *the tree.* It tells what happened: *grew taller.* It begins with a capital letter. It ends with a period.

Now You Try It

 2 Which is a sentence?

- ○ My sister ate her lunch.
- ○ Peanut butter and jelly.
- ○ Drank some milk.

Check your answer on page 109.

KNOW THE SKILL: **Periods**

A sentence that tells something ends with a period. Most sentences that give a command also end with a period. Here is one example: *Please pass the salt.*

Test Example

1 Write a punctuation mark to complete the sentence.

Mike was late for school

Think About the Answer

The sentence makes a statement so it needs a period.

Now You Try It

2 Write a sentence that ends with a period.

_____

Check your answer on page 109.

Language

KNOW THE SKILL: **Question Marks**

A question begins with a capital letter. It ends with a question mark. The order of the words in a question is different than a telling sentence.

Test Example

1 Choose the correct punctuation mark to complete this sentence:

Is the dog in the closet

- ○ .
- ○ ?
- ○ !

Think About the Answer

The sentence is a question so it should end with a question mark.

Now You Try It

2 Write a sentence that asks a question.

_____

Check your answer on page 109.

Advantage Test Prep Grade 1 © 2004 Creative Teaching Press

KNOW THE SKILL: **Exclamation Points**

A sentence that expresses strong feelings should end with an exclamation point.

Test Example

1. Which sentence ends correctly?

   ○ Watch out!

   ○ I was so scared.

   ○ Did you bring your math book home!

Think About the Answer

The first sentence is correct. It expresses strong feelings and ends with an exclamation point. The second sentence should end with an exclamation point. The third sentence should end with a question mark.

Now You Try It

2. Write a sentence that expresses a strong feeling.

_____

Check your answer on page 109.

KNOW THE SKILL: Capitalizing Names

The first word of a sentence should begin with a capital letter. Names of specific people, places, and things should also begin with capital letters. For example:

- Use a capital letter for *David*, but not *boy*.
- Use a capital for *Cleveland*, but not *city*.
- Use a capital for *Monday*, but not *day*.
- Use a capital for *June*, but not *month*.

Test Example

1 Which sentence is correct?

- ○ My Friend is moving to Kentucky.
- ○ My friend is moving to Kentucky.
- ○ My friend is moving to kentucky.

Think About the Answer

The second sentence uses capital letters correctly. In the first sentence, *Friend* should not begin with a capital. In the third sentence, *kentucky* should begin with a capital letter.

Now You Try It

2 Which sentence is correct?

- ○ His birthday is in july.
- ○ His birthday is in July.
- ○ His Birthday is in July.

Check your answer on page 109.

Advantage Test Prep Grade 1 © 2004 Creative Teaching Press

Language

KNOW THE SKILL: **Nouns**

A noun is the name of a person, a place, or a thing. There can be more than one noun in a sentence.

Test Example

1 Which is the noun?

That story was exciting.

- ○ was
- ○ story
- ○ exciting

Think About the Answer

Story is the noun in the sentence. A story is a thing. *Was* is a verb and *exciting* is a describing word. They are not nouns.

Now You Try It

2 Write the nouns on the lines.

The girl hit the ball, which flew through the air.

_____

_____

_____

Check your answer on page 109.

KNOW THE SKILL: **Describing Words**

Describing words tell about nouns. They might tell what the noun looks like or sounds like. They could tell how the noun feels, smells, or tastes. A sentence can have more than one describing word.

Test Example

1 Which word describes?

Madison saw a black dog.

○ Madison

○ black

○ dog

Think About the Answer

Black is the describing word. *Black* describes *dog*. *Madison* and *dog* are both nouns.

Now You Try It

2 Draw a line under the describing word and circle the word it describes.

Red flowers grew in the garden.

Check your answer on page 109.

Advantage Test Prep Grade 1 © 2004 Creative Teaching Press

Language

KNOW THE SKILL: **Verbs**

Many verbs are action words, such as *jump* and *talk*. They tell what nouns do. Other verbs connect a noun with a describing word. Here is an example: Joey *is* tired. *Is* is a verb that connects *Joey* (a noun) with *tired* (a describing word).

Test Example

1 Choose the verb in this sentence:

The spaghetti was hot.

- ○ hot
- ○ spaghetti
- ○ was

Think About the Answer

Was is the verb. It connects the noun *spaghetti* with the describing word *hot.*

Now You Try It

2 Write the verbs in these sentences on the lines.

Our team won the game. _____

We were the champs! _____

We yelled and cheered. _____ _____

Check your answer on page 109.

KNOW THE SKILL: **Present Tense**

The tense of a verb tells when something happened. A present tense verb describes something happening right now: *talk, paint, cry, sleep.*

Test Example

1. Choose the sentence that says that something is happening right now.

- ○ I am practicing my karate moves.
- ○ I practiced my karate moves.
- ○ I will practice my karate moves tomorrow.

Think About the Answer

The first sentence is the answer. The second sentence is about something that already happened. The third sentence is about something that will happen in the future.

Now You Try It

2. Write a sentence about something that is happening right now.

_____

_____

Check your answer on page 109.

Grammar and Usage

Language

KNOW THE SKILL: **Past Tense**

Verbs that say something already happened are past tense. Many past tense verbs end in *-ed*.

Test Example

1. Choose the sentence that says that something has already happened.
   - ○ My grandmother calls me.
   - ○ My grandmother called me.
   - ○ My grandmother will call me.

Think About the Answer

The second sentence is the answer. The verb *called* means that the grandmother already did it. The first sentence is about something that is happening now. The third sentence is about something that will happen in the future.

Now You Try It

2. Write the past tense of the word *open* on the line to show that something already happened.

   I _____ the present.

Check your answer on page 109.

Language

KNOW THE SKILL: **Complete and Incomplete Sentences**

A complete sentence tells a complete thought. It has a noun that tells what or who the sentence is about. It also has a verb that tells what happened. A complete sentence begins with a capital letter. It ends with a period, a question mark, or an exclamation point.

Test Example

1. Which is a sentence?
   - ○ James likes pizza best of all.
   - ○ His favorite food.
   - ○ Best of all.

Think About the Answer

The first sentence is complete. It has a noun, *James.* It has a verb, *likes.* It begins with a capital letter. It ends with a period. The second sentence does not have a verb. The third sentence does not have a noun.

Now You Try It

2. Which is NOT a sentence?
   - ○ My class.
   - ○ We went to the park.
   - ○ My class went to the park.

Check your answer on page 110.

KNOW THE SKILL: **Singular and Plural Nouns**

A singular noun names one person, place, or thing. A plural noun names more than one person, place, or thing. To make a noun plural, we usually add -s: *dog* becomes *dogs.*

Test Example

1. Write the plural of the word *book* on the line to finish the sentence.

The _____ were on the table.

Think About the Answer

Did you write *books*? The plural of *book* is *books.*

Now You Try It

2. Write the plural of the word sheet on the line to finish the sentence.

We handed in our answer _____.

Check your answer on page 110.

Language

KNOW THE SKILL: **Possessives**

To show that something belongs to someone, you make a noun possessive. To make a singular noun possessive, add an apostrophe and an s: the *dog's* dish. Many plural nouns already end with s. To make a plural noun possessive, add an apostrophe after the final s: the *teachers'* room.

Test Example

1. Write the possessive of the word *friend* on the line to complete the sentence.

   I stopped at my _____ house.

Think About the Answer

The answer is *friend's. Friend* is singular, so you add *'s* to show possession.

Now You Try It

2. Which word correctly completes the sentence?

   She looked in the _____ nest.

   ○ birds's

   ○ birds'

   ○ birds

Check your answer on page 110.

Language

KNOW THE SKILL: **Spelling the /k/ Sound**

The /k/ sound can be spelled with *k (keep)*, *c (care)*, or *ck (rock)*. On a test, spell the word on scrap paper before you look at the choices. Then choose the correct answer.

Test Example

1 Choose the word that is spelled correctly.

○ clown

○ klown

○ cklown

Think About the Answer

The first choice is the correct spelling. In this word, the /k/ sound is spelled with a *c*.

Now You Try It

2 Choose the sentence without a spelling mistake.

○ I need to go to the doktor.

○ The dog chased the stik.

○ Is that a snake?

Check your answer on page 110.

Language

KNOW THE SKILL: **Spelling Common Words**

When you are asked to spell a common word, write the word on scrap paper first, before you look at the choices. Then choose the correct answer.

Test Example

1 Which word is spelled correctly?
- ○ squirel
- ○ squirrel
- ○ skuirrel

Think About the Answer

The second spelling is correct.

Now You Try It

2 Which word is spelled correctly?
- ○ chilren
- ○ children
- ○ childern

Check your answer on page 110.

Advantage Test Prep Grade 1 © 2004 Creative Teaching Press

Introduction to Mathematics

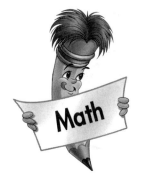

Mathematics is a language. You use it when you buy, measure, cook, build, count, and use a calendar. An understanding of mathematics helps students solve problems and comprehend ideas. Most standardized tests have math sections that address a broad range of skills.

By studying this section of the workbook, students will develop math skills. This will help them understand and use math better on tests and in all that they do.

- Writing Numbers
- Comparisons
- Number Order
- Counting On to Add
- Counting Back to Subtract
- Fact Families
- Ordinal Numbers
- Odd and Even Numbers
- Number Sentences
- Place Value
- Counting Dimes, Nickels, and Pennies
- Estimating
- Comparing Shapes
- Counting Sides
- Symmetry
- Measuring Length
- Measuring Weight
- Telling Time
- Number Patterns
- Bar Graphs
- Making a Plan
- Showing Your Work

Number Sense and Numeration

KNOW THE SKILL: **Counting**

When you count, you can write a number to show how many things there are.

How many baseballs? There are 5 baseballs!

Test Example

1   How many cakes?

- ○ 5
- ○ 4
- ○ 6
- ○ 8

Think About the Answer

There are eight cakes. Fill in the bubble next to the 8 with your pencil.

Now You Try It

2   How many bicycles?

- ○ 5
- ○ 6
- ○ 8
- ○ 9

Check your answer on page 110.

Advantage Test Prep Grade 1 © 2004 Creative Teaching Press

Number Sense and Numeration

Math

KNOW THE SKILL: **Which Is More?**

Look at two numbers. Which number is more? Which number is less? Look at two groups. Which has more?

Test Example

(1) How many triangles △ ? _____

How many squares ☐ ? _____

Which group has more? _____

Think About the Answer

There are 8 triangles. There are 5 squares. There are more triangles.

Now You Try It

(2) How many diamonds? _____

How many crescent moons? _____

Which group has more? _____

Check your answer on page 110.

Number Sense and Numeration

KNOW THE SKILL: **Number Order**

When you see a number, you can tell what numbers come *before* and *after* it. When you see two numbers, you should be able to tell what numbers come in between.

Test Example

1. Which number belongs in the blank space?

   4, 5, 6, _____, 8

   ○ 6
   ○ 7
   ○ 9
   ○ 8

Think About the Answer

The number 7 goes in the blank. It is the number *between* 6 and 8.

Now You Try It

2. Write the number that comes *before* 6. _____

Check your answer on page 110.

Advantage Test Prep Grade 1 © 2004 Creative Teaching Press

KNOW THE SKILL: **Counting On to Add**

Counting on is a skill you can use to add more to a number you already have. When you count on to a number, you make it that much bigger. Here's an example:

Here are five beans. 1 2 3 4 5

And you add two more beans.

You keep counting two more numbers: 6, 7. Now there are *seven* beans.

Test Example

1 Here are four blocks.

How much is three more blocks?

○ 6   ○ 9
○ 7   ○ 8

Think About the Answer

Start with 4 and count up three more—5, 6, 7.

Now You Try It

2 Here are five cups.

How much is three more cups?

○ 6   ○ 9
○ 7   ○ 8

Check your answer on page 110.

KNOW THE SKILL: Counting Back to Subtract

Counting back is a skill you use to take away from a number. When you count back, you make the number smaller. Here's an example:

Let's say we have six scooters.

If you take away two scooters, four scooters are left.

Test Example

1. Here are eight soccer balls.

How many is two fewer?

- ○ 6
- ○ 7
- ○ 9
- ○ 8

Think About the Answer

We started with eight and lost two. 8 − 2 = 6.

Now You Try It

2. Here are nine stars.

How many is three fewer?

- ○ 3
- ○ 1
- ○ 2
- ○ 6

Check your answer on page 110.

Advantage Test Prep Grade 1 © 2004 Creative Teaching Press

KNOW THE SKILL: **Fact Families**

The numbers 3, 2, and 5 make a fact family. These same numbers can be added or subtracted four different ways:

Addition	Subtraction
$3 + 2 = 5$	$5 - 2 = 3$
$2 + 3 = 5$	$5 - 3 = 2$

Test Example

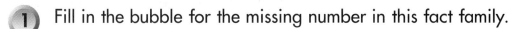

1 Fill in the bubble for the missing number in this fact family.

$$3 + 2 = 5 \qquad 5 - 2 = 3$$
$$2 + 3 = 5 \qquad 5 - \square = 2$$

○ 2   ○ 5   ○ 3   ○ 8

Think About the Answer

The missing number is 3 because $5 - 3 = 2$. The other numbers do not belong in the box.

Now You Try It

2 Fill in the bubble for the missing number in this fact family.

$$1 + 3 = \square \qquad 4 - 1 = 3$$
$$3 + 1 = 4 \qquad 4 - 3 = 1$$

○ 1   ○ 3   ○ 4   ○ 6

Check your answer on page 110.

KNOW THE SKILL: **Ordinal Numbers**

We use words to show the order of things. In this train, each car has a number. The first car is number 1, the second car is number 2, the third car is number 3, and so on.

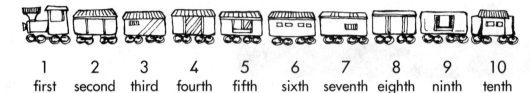

1	2	3	4	5	6	7	8	9	10
first	second	third	fourth	fifth	sixth	seventh	eighth	ninth	tenth

Test Example

1 Draw a circle around the fourth snowman.

Think About the Answer

To find the fourth snowman, begin on the left and count to four. The snowman you count last is the fourth one. That is the one you should circle.

Now You Try It

2 Draw a line through the sixth circle.

Check your answer on page 110.

Advantage Test Prep Grade 1 © 2004 Creative Teaching Press

KNOW THE SKILL: **Odd and Even Numbers**

The numbers 1, 3, 5, 7, and 9 are called **odd** numbers; 0, 2, 4, 6, and 8 are called **even** numbers.

Test Example

1 Which is odd?

○ 1 ○ 8 ○ 4 ○ 6

Think About the Answer

1 is the correct answer. The numbers 8, 4, and 6 are all even numbers.

Now You Try It

2 Which is even?

○ 3 ○ 6 ○ 9 ○ 5

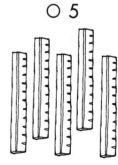

Check your answer on page 110.

Computation, Operations, Estimation

KNOW THE SKILL: **Number Sentences**

When you put together numbers in a number sentence, you can show what happens when they are added together or subtracted from each other.

Test Example

1 Write a number sentence for this story.

There are 5 .

4 more join them.

How many are there now?

_____ + _____ = _____

Think About the Answer

There are five birds. Four more join them. 5 + 4 = 9.

Now You Try It

2 Write a number sentence for this story.

Luis has 7 .

His brother gives him 3 .

How many does he have in all?

_____ + _____ = _____

Check your answer on page 110.

Advantage Test Prep Grade 1 © 2004 Creative Teaching Press

KNOW THE SKILL: **Which Sign?**

If you see a number sentence with a sign missing, can you figure out which sign belongs in the blank? You know that

+ means **add**

− means **take away.**

Test Example

1. Write the missing sign on the line.

7 _____ 2 = 9

Think About the Answer

The missing sign is +. If the sign were − , the difference would be 5. Since the answer is 9, it must be an addition number sentence.

Now You Try It

2. Write the missing sign on the line.

5 _____ 3 = 8

Check your answer on page 110.

KNOW THE SKILL: **Place Value**

Numbers can be shown with 10's blocks:

and with 1's blocks:

Test Example

1 What number is this?

○ 2
○ 12
○ 10
○ 14

Think about the Answer

The answer is 12. There are ten blocks in the top row and two more on the bottom. 10 + 2 = 12.

Now You Try It

2 What number is this?

○ 6
○ 14
○ 15
○ 5

Check your answer on page 110.

Advantage Test Prep Grade 1 © 2004 Creative Teaching Press

KNOW THE SKILL: **Counting Dimes, Nickels, and Pennies**

Learn how to tell the value of a group of coins. When you see pictures of coins together, count them like real money to find out how much they are worth.

Test Example

1. How much money is this?

   ○ 9 cents

   ○ 5 cents

   ○ 4 cents

   ○ 8 cents

Think About the Answer

The first answer is correct.

5 cents + 1 cent + 1 cent + 1 cent + 1 cent = 9 cents.

Now You Try It

2. How much money is this?

   ○ 6 cents

   ○ 19 cents

   ○ 15 cents

   ○ 5 cents

Check your answer on page 110.

Math

KNOW THE SKILL: **Estimating**

Estimating is making a smart guess about how many things there are in a group without counting.

Test Example

1 Estimate which group is bigger.

- ○ squares
- ○ circles
- ○ neither
- ○ I can't tell

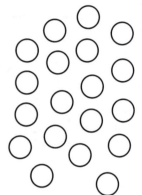

Think About the Answer

Ask yourself: Which group looks bigger to my eyes? The second answer is correct. The group of circles is larger.

Now You Try It

2 Estimate which group is bigger.

- ○ stars
- ○ triangles
- ○ neither
- ○ I can't tell

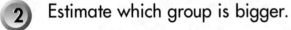

Check your answer on page 110.

Advantage Test Prep Grade 1 © 2004 Creative Teaching Press

KNOW THE SKILL: **Comparing Shapes**

When you compare shapes, look at them to see if they are alike or different.

Test Example

1 Which shape does NOT belong?

○   ○   ○   ○

Think About the Answer

The circle does not belong. The other shapes are squares and rectangles. They are made of lines with no curves. The circle is the only shape with a curve.

Now You Try It

2 Which shape does NOT belong?

             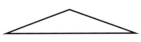

○   ○   ○   ○

Check your answer on page 110.

KNOW THE SKILL: **Counting Sides**

When you see a shape, you can tell what shape it is by counting how many flat sides it has.

A triangle has 3 sides.   A square has 4 sides.   A pentagon has 5 sides.   A hexagon has 6 sides.

Test Example

1. How many sides does this shape have?

   ○ 4
   ○ 2
   ○ 3
   ○ 5

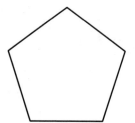

Think About the Answer

You can see that this is a 5-sided pentagon. It has one more side than a square.

Now You Try It

2. What is the name of this figure?

   ○ square
   ○ circle
   ○ triangle
   ○ pentagon

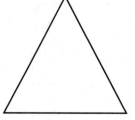

Check your answer on page 110.

Advantage Test Prep Grade 1 © 2004 Creative Teaching Press

KNOW THE SKILL: **Symmetry**

A circle is symmetrical. You can cut a circle out of paper and fold it in half. The halves will match exactly. Other shapes are also symmetrical. Imagine a line cutting the drawing you are looking at in half. If both parts match, it is symmetrical.

Test Example

1 Which of these shapes is symmetrical?

○   ○   ○   ○

Think About the Answer

The guitar is symmetrical. The shape is the same on both sides of the line. The other shapes are different on both sides of the line.

Now You Try It

2 Which of these shapes is NOT symmetrical.

○   ○   ○   ○

Check your answer on page 110.

KNOW THE SKILL: **Measuring Length**

Learn about different units of measure, such as inches, feet, and centimeters.

an inch is about this long: —— 1 inch ——

a centimeter is about this long: 1 centimeter ——

a foot is about as tall as this page

Test Example

1   How long is your eye?

○ about 1 foot

○ longer than 1 foot

○ shorter than 1 foot

○ shorter than 1 centimeter

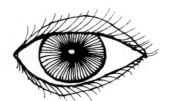

Think About the Answer

The correct answer is shorter than 1 foot. An eye is nowhere near a foot long, but it is bigger than 1 centimeter.

Now You Try It

2   How long is your arm?

○ about 1 foot

○ longer than 1 foot

○ shorter than 1 foot

○ shorter than 1 inch

Check your answer on page 110.

Advantage Test Prep Grade 1 © 2004 Creative Teaching Press

Measurement

KNOW THE SKILL: **Measuring Weight**

Practice using a scale to see how heavy things are and how heavy a pound is. Then, you can compare weights using words such as *lighter*, *heavier*, and *about*.

Test Example

1. How heavy is a pencil? Choose the best answer.
   - ○ lighter than 1 pound
   - ○ heavier than 1 pound
   - ○ about 1 pound
   - ○ heavier than you

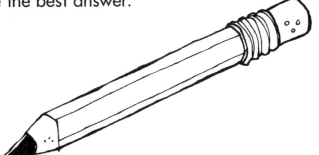

Think About the Answer

The correct answer is lighter than 1 pound. A pencil is very light. It could fit in your hand. It would not weigh anywhere close to a pound. It could never weigh as much as a person.

Now You Try It

2. How heavy is a dog? Choose the best answer.
   - ○ lighter than 1 pound
   - ○ heavier than 1 pound
   - ○ about 1 pound
   - ○ lighter than a pencil

Check your answer on page 110.

KNOW THE SKILL: **Telling Time**

You should be able to tell what time it is by looking at a clock. On a clock the little hand tells you what hour it is.

Test Example

1. What time is it on this clock?
   - ○ 2:00
   - ○ 8:00
   - ○ 12:00
   - ○ 3:00

Think About the Answer

The little hand on the clock is pointing at the 3 so the time is 3:00.

Now You Try It

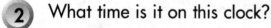

2. What time is it on this clock?
   - ○ 3:00
   - ○ 10:00
   - ○ 9:00
   - ○ 12:00

Check your answer on page 111.

KNOW THE SKILL: **Number Patterns**

You can see patterns in a line of shapes, letters, or numbers. Once you see the pattern, you may be asked to draw or write what comes next.

Test Example

1 Draw what comes next.

Think About the Answer

You should have drawn a white circle. The pattern goes back and forth between white circles and black circles. Since the last one was a black circle, the next one is a white circle.

Now You Try It

2 Draw what comes next.

Check your answer on page 111.

KNOW THE SKILL: **Reading a Graph**

A **graph** is a way to show information about a lot of people at once. Each line in the chart shown below tells you how many of each pet the 1st graders liked the best.

Test Example

1 What pet did the most children like?

- ○ cats
- ○ dogs
- ○ guinea pigs
- ○ other pets

Our Favorite Pets

Cats	🐱 🐱 🐱 🐱 🐱 🐱
Dogs	🐶 🐶 🐶 🐶 🐶
Guinea Pigs	🐹 🐹 🐹
Other Pets	🐍 🐟 🐟

Think About the Answer

Cats is the correct answer. Six children like cats the best. All the other pets got fewer votes.

Now You Try It

2 How many 1st graders liked guinea pigs the best? _____

Check your answer on page 111.

Advantage Test Prep Grade 1 © 2004 Creative Teaching Press

Problem Solving

KNOW THE SKILL: Making a Plan

When solving word problems, look for these key words:

altogether means to add up numbers

more means to add a number

less means to subtract a number

take away means to subtract a number

Test Example

1. Choose the number sentence for this word problem:

Dan had 4 stickers. His friend Jamal gave him 8 <u>more</u>. How many did Dan have <u>altogether</u>?

- ○ 4 – 4 = ?
- ○ 8 + 8 = ?
- ○ 4 + 8 = ?
- ○ 8 – 4 = ?

Think About the Answer

The problem says Dan had 4 stickers and Jamal gave him 8 more. That means that the choice of 4 + 8 = ? is correct. It will give us the answer to the word problem.

Now You Try It

2. Choose the number sentence for this word problem:

Our class went on two buses. One bus had 12 students. The other bus had 9 students. How many students went <u>altogether</u>?

- ○ 12 – 9 = ?
- ○ 12 + 2 = ?
- ○ 12 + 9 = ?
- ○ 9 – 9 = ?

Check your answer on page 111.

Problem Solving

KNOW THE SKILL: **Showing Your Work**

You can write words and numbers and pictures on paper to solve math problems. This is called showing your work. It helps you think and shows others how you think, too.

Test Example

1 Choose the number sentence that matches this picture:

x x x + o o o o = 7

- ○ 7 – 7 = 7
- ○ 4 – 3 = 7
- ○ 3 + 4 = 7
- ○ 7 + 7 = 7

Think About the Answer

There are 3 x's and 4 o's. When added together, they equal 7. The math sentence 3 + 4 = 7 is the answer.

Now You Try It

2 Write a number sentence to match this picture:

o o o o o ᴏ̶ ᴏ̶

_____

Check your answer on page 111.

Advantage Test Prep Grade 1 © 2004 Creative Teaching Press

Practice Test Introduction

This practice test is like a real test students take at school. It will help students see if they know all the skills they have studied in this book. The questions in the test are similar to the ones students already practiced in previous pages.

The test is divided into the same sections as the earlier parts of the book. There are sections on reading, writing, language arts, and math. Here are some tips for students to keep in mind during the practice test:

- These tests are meant to be a challenge for you. See how you do.

- Read the directions carefully before you start.

- If you have any questions, ask an adult.

- The practice test has no time limit. Still, work as quickly as you can. That will help you practice for taking tests in school.

- Try to finish each section in one session. You will see a stop sign at the end of the section.

- If you don't know an answer, come back to the question later.

- After you finish each section, check your answers. The answers begin on page 111.

Read the story. Then answer questions 1 through 10.

The Dinosaur Box

"Can I have the box?" Grace asked. Her family just bought a new clothes washer. It came in a huge box.

"Sure," Dad said. "Have fun!"

One side of the box was open. Grace looked inside. It was too empty. She would fix that. Grace found her crayons. Soon the inside was covered with pictures. Grace drew her favorite thing—dinosaurs.

Then Grace yawned. Drawing dinosaurs makes you tired. Suddenly, Grace felt something wet on her hand.

Grace grabbed her hand away from the wet thing. It looked like a giant tongue! How could that be? Then she peeked outside the box. A dinosaur was standing there! "What are you doing here?" Grace asked.

"Why, I live here," the dinosaur said. "What are you doing here?"

Grace got out of the box and looked around. She was in a jungle! "Where am I? How did I get here?" she asked.

GO

Advantage Test Prep Grade 1 © 2004 Creative Teaching Press

"Why, you came in that box, I think," the dinosaur said. Then he turned and listened. "Wait! I just heard something!"

Grace heard it, too. It was a low sound, but it was a little like a roar. The next one was much louder. It shook the ground!

"What . . . what is that?" she whispered.

The dinosaur's eyes were big. "It's T-Rex! He's hungry again! I've got to get out of here!"

"Wait! What about me?" Grace asked. "Where should I go?"

"I'd get back in that box if I were you," the dinosaur said. He rushed into the jungle. Grace hurried into the box. She pulled it shut and hugged herself.

Then she heard another sound. "Grace, come out of that box!" Was T-Rex talking to her? How did he know her name?

Then Grace saw a hand pulling the box open. Was T-Rex going to get her?

"Come on, sleepyhead," Mom said. "It's past your bedtime."

GO

1 Was this story real or make-believe?

     ○ It was real.

     ○ It was make-believe.

     ○ There is no way to tell.

2 Which happened FIRST?

     ○   ○   ○

3 Which word correctly completes the sentence?

One dinosaur in the story is friendly, and one is _____.

     ○ scary

     ○ small

     ○ hungry

4 What does this story tell you about life?

     ○ Playing in boxes is dangerous.

     ○ Don't be afraid of dinosaurs.

     ○ Dreams can seem very real.

5 How did Grace get away from T-Rex?

_____

Advantage Test Prep Grade 1 © 2004 Creative Teaching Press

6 How did the first dinosaur know that T-Rex was coming?

_____

7 Where did Grace hide?

○ with a fox   ○ inside a box   ○ in some socks

8 What will Mom do when Grace tells her about the dinosaurs?

○   ○   ○

9 What was the main idea of the story?

　　○ Grace dreamed about some dinosaurs.

　　○ Grace almost was eaten by T-Rex.

　　○ Grace fell asleep in a big box.

10 What did you like about this story? Give reasons for your answer.

_____

_____

_____

_____

GO →

Read the passage and look at the map. Then answer questions 11 through 20.

Dinosaur National Monument

Dinosaur National Monument is in the West. It is in Colorado and Utah. This park has many dinosaur bones.

Many years ago, a river ran through this park. Dinosaurs lived near the river. When they died, some of them slipped into the river. Sand covered their bones. It buried them.

The buried bones turned into rock. Now they are fossils.

The river dried up. In 1909, a man found some of the bones. More people came to dig. They found bones from 11 kinds of dinosaurs.

The dinosaurs died long ago. All we have left are their bones.

Scientists study the bones. They put them back together. They learn what the dinosaurs looked like.

At the park, you can see a special wall. It is cut into a hill. It still has 1,500 dinosaur bones in it. They are still sticking out of the sand and rock.

Many of the bones at this park are from one kind of dinosaur. It was the biggest dinosaur to walk on land. Some of these dinosaurs weighed 34 tons!

If you go to Dinosaur National Monument, you might find a dinosaur bone!

11 Which group do dinosaurs belong in?

    ○   ○   ○

12 Which happened LAST?

    ○ The park opened.

    ○ The dinosaurs died.

    ○ The bones turned into rock.

13 What do you think will happen at the park?

    ○ Someone will find a live dinosaur.

    ○ People will find more bones.

    ○ More dinosaurs will die.

14 Which phrase correctly completes the sentence?

The first bone was found at the park _____.

    ○ 150 million years ago

    ○ in 1909

    ○ in 2003

15 Did all dinosaur bones turn into fossils?

_____

Advantage Test Prep Grade 1 © 2004 Creative Teaching Press

16 Which state is north of the park?

○ Utah

○ Colorado

○ Wyoming

17 Which state is at the east end of the park?

_____

18 Which phrase correctly completes the sentence?

A dinosaur is like a person because _____.

○ they are both about the same size

○ they both have bones

○ they are both alive

19 What is the main idea in this passage?

○ Dinosaur bones can turn into fossils.

○ We do not know why the dinosaurs all died.

○ You can see many dinosaur bones at this park.

20 Would Dinosaur National Monument be a good place to visit? Why or why not?

_____

_____

_____

STOP

Practice Test: Writing

Writing Prompt

Tell about a time when you made a good decision. Here are some ideas to get you started:

- Maybe you decided to finish a project instead of watching television.

- Maybe you wished you hadn't done something, but you decided to admit you did.

- Maybe you decided to make or buy something for a friend instead of for yourself.

- Maybe you decided to visit an older person instead of playing with your friends.

- You can think of other ideas yourself.

Writers' Checklist

Make sure you do all these things as you write:

☐ I explained my choices.

☐ I told which choice I made.

☐ I explained why.

☐ I told what I did or what happened after my decision.

☐ I explained why that was a good decision.

☐ I used enough details to make my ideas clear.

☐ I put my ideas in order so the reader can understand what happened.

☐ I spelled first-grade spelling words correctly.

☐ I started names and the first word of each sentence with a capital letter.

☐ My sentences are complete. They end with a period, a question mark, or an exclamation point.

Advantage Test Prep Grade 1 © 2004 Creative Teaching Press

Plan Your Writing

Use this page to plan your writing. You might use listing or webbing. You might have another way to get started.

_____

_____

_____

_____

_____

_____

GO →

Write Your First Draft

Use all the skills you have learned to write a first draft.

_____

_____

_____

_____

_____

_____

_____

_____

_____

_____

_____

_____

Advantage Test Prep Grade 1 © 2004 Creative Teaching Press

Write Your Final Draft

Now it's time to write your final draft. Read the writer's checklist on page 88 again. Make sure you did all the things on the checklist. Look for other ways to make your writing clearer.

_____

_____

_____

_____

_____

_____

_____

_____

_____

_____

_____

GO

_____

_____

_____

_____

_____

Scoring Yourself

Go back to the writing rubric on page 31. Give yourself a score from 4 to 0 for each category. Then ask someone else to score your writing. Then you will have two scores.

How I Scored It

Ideas	Organization	Sentence Structure	Spelling, Punctuation, and Grammar
_____	_____	_____	_____

How Someone Else Scored It

Ideas	Organization	Sentence Structure	Spelling, Punctuation, and Grammar
_____	_____	_____	_____

21 Which sentence is complete?

   ○ We had fun at the play.

   ○ Tina, Mandy, and me.

   ○ Tuesday afternoon.

22 Which sentence has the correct end mark?

   ○ Where are you going.

   ○ He went along, too.

   ○ Look out.

23 Choose the end mark that correctly completes this sentence:

Is that your backpack

   ○ ?

   ○ !

   ○ .

24 Choose the sentence with the correct end mark.

   ○ I won the contest!

   ○ I filled out the form!

   ○ Did you enter the contest!

25 Write a sentence about an event at your school. Name your school in the sentence. Use capital letters correctly.

_____

Advantage Test Prep Grade 1 © 2004 Creative Teaching Press

26 Circle the noun in this sentence:

That horse looks hungry.

27 Circle the describing word in this sentence:

It ate the yellow flowers.

28 Circle the verb in this sentence:

The flowers tasted good.

29 Write the past tense of *learn* on the line to the complete sentence.

Yesterday, we _____about zoos.

30 Which sentence tells about something that is happening now?

     ○ Charles talks about his turtle.

     ○ Charles talked about his turtle.

     ○ Charles will talk about his turtle.

31 Which sentence is complete?

   ○ Our class rode a bus to the park.

   ○ Brought our lunches.

   ○ A bus to the park

32 Which word completes this sentence correctly?

Ricky brought two _____ to school.

   ○ snake

   ○ snakes

   ○ snake's

33 Which word completes this sentence correctly?

One snake crawled under _____ desk.

   ○ Rickys

   ○ Rickys'

   ○ Ricky's

34 Which sentence has the correct end mark?

   ○ I heard someone whisper?

   ○ Do you hear a noise?

   ○ Listen?

35 Which option should replace the underlined portion of the sentence?

Are you coming with <u>us!</u>

   ○ us?

   ○ us,

   ○ us.

GO →

36 Which sentence has the correct end mark?

    ○ We love ice cream!

    ○ Who wants ice cream!

    ○ Can I have a cone, please!

37 Which sentence uses capital letters correctly?

    ○ Sharla went to the doctor on Tuesday.

    ○ Sharla went to the Doctor on tuesday.

    ○ Sharla went to the Doctor on Tuesday.

38 Circle the two nouns in this sentence:

Dogs make great pets.

39 Circle the describing word in this sentence:

My dog Barky has the blackest fur.

40 Circle the verb in this sentence:

Barky chases my cat all of the time.

GO →

41 Which sentence tells about something that already happened?

    ○ It is your turn.

    ○ I liked your book report.

    ○ The teacher will call the next person.

42 Which sentence tells about something that is happening now?

    ○ The door slammed shut.

    ○ The woman smiled at me.

    ○ The woman opens the door.

43 Which word completes the sentence correctly?

We will need four more _____.

    ○ chair

    ○ chairs

    ○ chaires

44 Which word completes the sentence correctly?

I am trying out for the _____ softball team.

    ○ boys

    ○ boy's

    ○ boys'

45 Write a complete sentence. Be sure to use correct capitalization and punctuation.

_____

STOP

46 How many puppies?

○ 2   ○ 4
○ 7   ○ 8

47 How many tulips?

○ 3   ○ 8
○ 7   ○ 4

48 How many?

There are _____ ◯ . There are _____ ◇ .

There are more _____.

49 Which number belongs in the blank space?

2, 3, 4, _____, 6

○ 5   ○ 4   ○ 6   ○ 9

50 How many?

There are _____ ☐ . There are _____ ⬭ .

There are more _____.

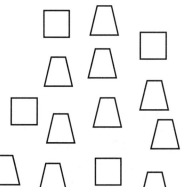

51 Which number belongs in the blank space?

7, 8, 9, _____, 11

○ 9   ○ 10   ○ 11   ○ 12

52 Which number belongs in the blank space?

14, _____, 16, 17, 18

○ 12   ○ 13   ○ 14   ○ 15

53 Here are seven stars.
How much is four more?

○ 7   ○ 4   ○ 11   ○ 10

54 Here are twelve sea shells.
How many is four fewer?

○ 12   ○ 8   ○ 11   ○ 9

55 Here are eight tennis balls.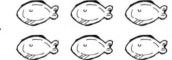
How many is two fewer?

○ 2   ○ 3   ○ 4   ○ 6

56 Here are six pieces of candy shaped like fish.
How much is one more?

○ 7   ○ 2   ○ 5   ○ 6

          Advantage Test Prep Grade 1 © 2004 Creative Teaching Press

57 Complete this fact family for the numbers 5, 4, and 9.

$$5 + 4 = 9 \qquad\qquad \underline{} - \underline{} = 5$$

$$\underline{} + \underline{} = 9 \qquad\qquad 9 - \underline{} = 4$$

58 Complete this fact family for the numbers 7, 6, and 13.

$$7 + 6 = 13 \qquad\qquad 13 - 6 = \underline{}$$

$$\underline{} + \underline{} = 13 \qquad\qquad \underline{} - 7 = \underline{}$$

59 Draw a circle around the third tree.

60 Draw a circle around the fifth violin.

61 Draw a circle around the eighth bunch of grapes.

62 Which is even?

    ○ 9   ○ 7   ○ 5   ○ 6

GO

63 Which is odd?

     ○ 8   ○ 16   ○ 11   ○ 6

64 Which is even?

     ○ 19   ○ 22   ○ 5   ○ 7

65 Write a number sentence for this story:
There are 8 ants. 2 more join them.
How many ants are there now?

_____ + _____ = _____ s.

66 Write a number sentence for this story.
There are 12 apples on the tree.
7 apples fall off the tree.
How many apples are there on the tree now?

_____ – _____ = _____ s.

67 Write the missing sign on the line.

1 ___ 4 = 5

68 Write the missing sign on the line.

9 ___ 3 = 12

GO →

Advantage Test Prep Grade 1 © 2004 Creative Teaching Press

69 Write the missing sign on the line.

14 ___ 6 = 8

70 What number is this?

| | | | | | | | | | |

| | | | | | | | | | | | | | | |

○ 24   ○ 14   ○ 22   ○ 16

71 What number is this?

| | | | | | | | | | |

| | | | | | | | | | |

| | | | | | | | | | | | | | | | | |

○ 34   ○ 26   ○ 44   ○ 37

72 How much money is this?

○ 11 cents   ○ 5 cents   ○ 10 cents   ○ 15 cents

73 How much money is this?

○ 16 cents   ○ 12 cents   ○ 10 cents   ○ 20 cents

74 How much money is this?

○ 21 cents   ○ 15 cents   ○ 23 cents   ○ 20 cents

75 Without counting, how many apples do you think there are?

- ○ about 20
- ○ about 30
- ○ about 10
- ○ about 50

76 Which shape does NOT belong?

  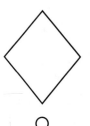 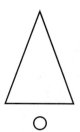

○   ○   ○   ○

77 How many triangles are there? _____

78 How many sides does this shape have?

- ○ 4   ○ 2
- ○ 3   ○ 5

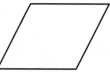

79 How many sides does this shape have?

- ○ 3   ○ 2
- ○ 6   ○ 5

Advantage Test Prep Grade 1 © 2004 Creative Teaching Press

80 Which of these shapes is symmetrical?

○   ○   ○   ○

81 How tall is a table?

    ○ about 3 feet   ○ about 3 inches

    ○ about 1 foot   ○ about 1 inch

82 How tall is a flower?

    ○ about 10 inches   ○ about 1 inch

    ○ about 10 feet   ○ about 5 feet

83 How heavy is a bicycle? Choose the best answer.

    ○ lighter than 1 pound

    ○ about 1 pound

    ○ heavier than 1 pound

    ○ lighter than a basketball

84 How heavy is a sandwich? Choose the best answer.

    ○ lighter than 1 pound

    ○ about 1 pound

    ○ heavier than 1 pound

    ○ heavier than a pair of boots

85 What time is it on this clock?

    ○ 1:00   ○ 6:00

    ○ 8:00   ○ 5:00

86 What time is it on this clock?

    ○ 12:00   ○ 10:00

    ○ 9:00   ○ 3:00

87 What time is it on this clock?

    ○ 7:00   ○ 5:00

    ○ 10:00   ○ 3:00

88 Draw what comes next.

X, X, Y, Y, X, X, Y, Y, X, X, _____

89 Draw what comes next.

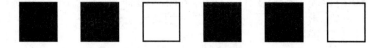

90 Draw what comes next.

Advantage Test Prep Grade 1 © 2004 Creative Teaching Press

Activities We Enjoy	
Baseball	⚾ ⚾ ⚾ ⚾ ⚾ ⚾ ⚾
Soccer	⚽ ⚽ ⚽ ⚽ ⚽ ⚽ ⚽ ⚽ ⚽
Swimming	🏊 🏊 🏊 🏊
Cycling	🚲 🚲

91 Read the chart above. What activity did the most people enjoy?

     ○ baseball   ○ soccer   ○ swimming   ○ cycling

92 What activity did the fewest people enjoy?

     ○ baseball   ○ soccer   ○ swimming   ○ cycling

93 How many more people play soccer than baseball?

     ○ 3   ○ 9   ○ 7   ○ 2

94 Make a number sentence for this word problem:

Jonathan read 6 books and Linda read 8 books. How many books did they read <u>altogether</u>?

_____

95 Choose the number sentence that matches this picture:

/ / / / / / + ○ ○ ○ ○ = 10

     ○ 5 + 5 = 10   ○ 6 − 4 = 2   ○ 6 + 4 = 10   ○ 7 + 3 = 10

Answer Key

Page 8

The answer is *cold.* The child is shivering because it's cold. The picture does not show warm or drop.

Page 9

The answer is *cool.* The ice cube is cool. The picture does not show a school or a tool.

Page 10

The answer is the first picture, rain falling from a cloud. The passage tells why rain falls. It does not mention playing in the ocean or watering plants.

Page 11

The first picture shows something that is make-believe. Real clouds do not cry. However, a child can fly a kite and rain does fall from clouds.

Page 12

similarity

Page 14

The first paragraph says that Luis is teaching his grandfather English.

Page 15

When Luis learns that rice and beans helped his mother grow, he wants to eat them, too.

Page 16

The correct answer is *family.* The people in the picture are all part of a family. The story does not say they are helpers. They live together, so they are not neighbors.

Page 17

The first picture was last. Luis hugs Mama at the end of the story. The other two pictures show things that happened earlier in the story.

Page 19

The first picture is the correct choice. She will probably go ahead and write the letter. She will do what needs to be done, no matter what. She will not stay in bed. Catching a bus is the answer for question 1, but it does not make sense here.

Page 20

The first picture is the correct answer. It shows someone who is determined. The poem does not suggest that the poet is sad or angry.

Page 21

Answers will vary. Students might like the positive attitude in the poem or the fact that it's tricky to say aloud. Others might think it is silly. Regardless, they should explain the reasons for their opinions.

Page 22

The correct answer is *The Pacific Ocean.* The United States is north. The Gulf of Mexico is east.

Page 23

The warmest day was Wednesday, when the temperature was 68.

Page 24

The correct answer is the third choice *Thursday, May 5.* There is no Tuesday, May 5. Tuesday, May 10, is a doctor's appointment.

Advantage Test Prep Grade 1 © 2004 Creative Teaching Press

Page 25

Line 5 asks for the name of a parent or guardian. Kim should write her mother's name, Jennifer Sampson.

Page 26

The correct answer is *pants, pen, phone, pig.* The words all start with *p,* so you put them in order by their second letters: *a, e, h, i.*

Page 27

The third set of guide words is correct. *Whistle* comes after *wheel* and before *wise,* so it would be on that page. *Whistle* comes after both *tool* and *tuna.* It also comes after both *warm* and *west. Whistle* would not be on those pages.

Page 28

Sketches will vary but should represent a stop sign. The stop sign should have 8 sides.

Page 29

Weather Experiments with Everyday Materials would probably show you how to do experiments with weather. The other books are about weather, but they do not seem to have experiments.

Page 40

The correct answer is the first choice, *My sister ate her lunch.* It names who the sentence is about (*my sister*) and what happened (*ate her lunch*). The second choice, *Peanut butter and jelly,* does not say what happened. The third choice, *Drank some milk,* does not tell who drank the milk.

Page 41

Sentences will vary, but they should end with a period. Here is one example: I *went to the store.*

Page 42

Questions will vary, but they should end with a question mark. Here is one example: *What is your name?*

Page 43

Exclamations will vary, but they should end with an exclamation point. Here is one example: *What a good time we had!*

Page 44

Only the second sentence is correct. The word *birthday* should not be capitalized because it is not the name of a certain day. *July* should be capitalized because it is the name of a certain month.

Page 45

girl, ball, air

Page 46

Red flowers grew in the garden.

Page 47

won
were
yelled, cheered

Page 48

Sentences will vary, but they should be in the present tense.

Page 49

The verb should be changed to past tense by adding *-ed:* I *opened* the present.

Page 50

The correct answer is the first choice. It is not a sentence. It has a noun but needs a verb. The second and third choices are complete sentences.

Page 51

We handed in our answer *sheets*. To make *sheet* plural, add *-s*.

Page 52

The correct answer is the second choice, *birds'*. The word *birds* is plural and ends in *-s,* so we just add an apostrophe.

Page 53

The third sentence has no mistakes. The /k/ sound in *snake* is spelled with a *k*. *Doktor* should be *doctor*. *Stik* should be *stick*.

Page 54

The second choice is correct. *Children* is often misspelled because people forget about the *d* or use *er* instead of *re*.

Page 56

6

Page 57

There are 6 diamonds. There are 4 moons. There are more diamonds.

Page 58

5

Page 59

8

Page 60

6

Page 61

4

Page 62

Page 63

6

Page 64

7 + 3 = 10

Page 65

The missing sign is a + sign.

Page 66

15

Page 67

19 cents

Page 68

The group of stars is bigger.

Page 69

The square does not belong.

Page 70

triangle

Page 71

The butter knife is not symmetrical.

Page 72

longer than 1 foot

Page 73

heavier than 1 pound

Advantage Test Prep Grade 1 © 2004 Creative Teaching Press

Page 74
12:00

Page 75
A circle comes next.

Page 76
3

Page 77
$12 + 9 = ?$

Page 78
$8 - 3 = 5$

Practice Test Answer Key
Reading
1 It was make-believe.
2 The third picture is correct. It shows a scene from the beginning of the story.
3 scary
4 Dreams can seem very real.
5 She woke up from her dream.
6 He heard T-Rex.
7 inside a box
8 The first picture is correct because Mom will smile.
9 Grace dreamed about some dinosaurs.
10 Answers will vary. Here is one example: *I liked the story because I like to read about dinosaurs.*
11 The third picture is correct. It shows a group of animals.
12 The park opened.
13 People will find more bones.
14 in 1909
15 No, just a few dinosaur bones turned into fossils.
16 Wyoming
17 Colorado
18 they both have bones
19 You can see many dinosaur bones at this park.
20 Answers will vary. Here is one possible answer: *It would be a good place to visit if you are interested in dinosaurs. You can see real bones that are still partly buried in a wall.*
21 We had fun at the play.
22 He went along, too.
23 ?
24 I won the contest!
25 Answers will vary. Answers should include proper use of capital letters. Here is one possible answer: *Each year, Dr. Jonas Salk Elementary School holds a spelling bee.*
26 horse
27 yellow
28 tasted
29 learned
30 Charles talks about his turtle.
31 Our class rode a bus to the park.
32 snakes
33 Ricky's
34 Do you hear a noise?
35 us?
36 We love ice cream!
37 Sharla went to the doctor on Tuesday.
38 Dogs, pets
39 blackest
40 chases
41 I liked your book report.
42 The woman opens the door.
43 chairs
44 boys'
45 Sentences will vary, but they should be complete and without errors.

Math
46 7

47　4

48　There are 8 circles. There are 5 diamonds. There are more circles.

49　5

50　There are 4 squares. There are 10 trapezoids. There are more trapezoids.

51　10

52　15

53　11

54　8

55　6

56　7

57　$5 + 4 = 9$　　$9 - 4 = 5$
　　$4 + 5 = 9$　　$9 - 5 = 4$

58　$7 + 6 = 13$　　$13 - 6 = 7$
　　$6 + 7 = 13$　　$13 - 7 = 6$

59　

60　

61　

62　6

63　11

64　22

65　$8 + 2 = 10$ ants.

66　$12 - 7 = 5$ apples.

67　The missing sign is a + sign.

68　The missing sign is a + sign.

69　The missing sign is a − sign.

70　24

71　37

72　15 cents

73　12 cents

74　21 cents

75　about 20

76　The triangle does not belong because it only has three sides. The other shapes have four sides.

77　5

78　4

79　6

80　The butterfly is the only shape that is symmetrical.

81　about three feet

82　about 10 inches

83　heavier than 1 pound

84　lighter than 1 pound

85　6:00

86　12:00

87　5:00

88　Y

89　

90　

91　soccer

92　cycling

93　2

94　$6 + 8 = 14$

95　$6 + 4 = 10$

Advantage Test Prep Grade 1 © 2004 Creative Teaching Press